Tickled by the Turning Tide

Tickled by the Turning Tide

The Folkestone Poems

Tony Quarrington

Patty

Enjoy!

Love

Tony x 23/4.

CONTENTS

CONTENTS

CONTENTS

Foreword

I first became aware of Tony's poetry after I was invited to give a talk to a Folkestone-based writers' group, of which he was a member. I soon recognised that Tony and I had a great deal in common. Not only do we share a love of poetry, but we have both found inspiration for our writing in our adopted seaside homes. For me, that is Whitstable which became the location for my crime novels. For Tony, the setting for his poetry lies some miles further down the Kent coast – in Folkestone.

Should you never have visited Folkestone you are about to explore this fascinating coastal area in the confident hands of an excellent guide. Along the way, you will find Tony's keen sense of observation in poems such as *Checkpoint George* – which details the clash between old and new town cultures – while Tony's wry humour is on display in *The Seagull's Breakfast*. Reverence and affection are conveyed in *Our Lady of the Harbour* – Tony's homage to the life-size mermaid sculpture – Folkestone's own version of Copenhagen's Little Mermaid – "rooted firmly on the East Head rocks staring intently out on mottled skies". *When the Young Boy Arrived*, a poem that pays its respects to Philip Larkin's *Annus Mirabilis* will, I am sure, allow you the chance to bask in a sense of warm nostalgia as comforting as a seaside nap in a deckchair on East Cliff Sands.

Walk with Tony as you turn these pages "down the steep, unforgiving hill, past higgledy-piggledy buildings that shelter the secrets of centuries.....Where restless waves wash over shingle, shifting the site of a billion pebbles, and where small, redundant, fishing boats, their hulls rotting and their history forgotten, are nudged and tickled by the turning tide.....".

These poems confirm that Folkestone is indeed *A Writer's Town* and Tony Quarrington its poetic chronicler.

Julie Wassmer
Author of *The Whitstable Pearl Mystery* novels
www.juliewassmer.com

Introduction

'Located on the south eastern coast of England, a handful of miles from the famed White Cliffs, and only twenty two miles from continental Europe, Folkestone has had a long, varied history, boasting both Bronze and Iron Age settlements and a prominent Roman Villa, sadly now perilously close to the cliff erosion that has always blighted this coastline.

Descended from the Anglo-Saxon Kings of Kent, Eanswythe, a devout young princess, founded a nunnery in the town in the seventh century AD, and was subsequently made a saint. Her bones, discovered in the parish church by workmen in 1885, were radiocarbon tested and confirmed in 2020, and the church is now a serious site of pilgrimage.

For a thousand years, Folkestone was a modest fishing village and, for most of that time, as a limb of the Cinque Port of Dover, also a busy trading port. Smuggling was a not insignificant business from the eighteenth century too. But it was the coming of the railway and associated cross-channel ferry industry from 1843, and the construction in later decades of grand hotels and white stuccoed family homes, notably in the West End, that contributed to its rise as a fashionable resort that attracted royalty, artists and writers in addition to the Victorian and Edwardian middle class.

Much of this development was conceived, funded and overseen by the Earl of Radnor, who still owns land in the town and surrounding area.

The "golden age" that began around 1880 arguably came to a sudden halt with the outbreak of the Great War, which had a profound effect on Folkestone. It became a major port of embarkation for the Western Front, and the final sight of England for millions of troops, many of whom will have marched from the neighbouring Shorncliffe army camp. The bombing of Tontine Street in 1917 brought about the highest number of British civilian dead as a result of an air raid during the war until that point.

The inter war years saw a revival, with Folkestone exploiting its natural beauty - the Channel views, rolling hills, delightful parks and gardens - by marketing itself as "Fashionable" and "Spacious and Gracious". Moreover, its popularity as a resort was enhanced by the Earl of Radnor's "foreshore development" that included the construction of the Rotunda, the largest unsupported concrete dome in Europe, swimming pool and boating lake, supplementing the existing Victoria Pier, switchback railway and 1885 Leas water lift.

The town suffered heavy bombardment during the Second World War, destroying much of the harbour, but recovered as a seaside destination during the fifties and early sixties, which is when my Folkestone story began.

The aforementioned Rotunda, quaint, steep Old High Street with the revered Rock and Joke shops and the popular ferry route to Boulogne-sur-Mer, kept the visitors coming and the locals entertained.

But, like so many other UK coastal resorts, it suffered a deep decline as the advent of cheap air fares, duty free and longer annual leave allowance, led to an escape to resorts where the sun was twenty degrees warmer and the beer ten degrees colder. Many beloved attractions and hotels closed, were demolished and converted into flats, and trade in the town slumped. Although the cross-channel ferry industry ceased at the turn of the century, Folkestone retained its role as a point of departure to the continent with the opening of the Channel Tunnel in 1994.

The new Millennium brought a revival, aided by the philanthropy of former Saga owner, Sir Roger De Haan, who renovated and refurbished many of the buildings in the old town, offering the properties to creatives at modest rents, provided education and sporting facilities (the latest of which the world's first multi-storey skatepark), and restored and remodelled the derelict harbour area. The construction of up to a thousand apartments along the shoreline between the Leas Lift (currently closed) and the Harbour Arm is also now underway.

Since 2008, the Triennial has showcased new works from established British and international artists. Around half of each event's pieces remain outdoors in the town once the exhibition is over. There are now around ninety on public display.

De Haan's influence and the arrival of the high speed rail link (less than an hour from London) in 2007, has proved a happy marriage in rendering Folkestone more accessible. Comparatively cheap (but rising) house prices, the advantages of living by the sea, a vibrant dining scene and improving facilities, not least for children, have all led to a growing relocation of people, many of them young families, predominantly from London.

My fondness for Folkestone began at the age of ten when I was brought by my parents from my hometown of Rochester, forty fives miles away on the North Kent coast, on the first of a succession of summer holidays to the town. It was my mother's admitted but modest pretensions to social mobility which led to the choice of Folkestone rather than the traditional "bucket and spade" resorts such as Herne Bay, Margate, Broadstairs or, closer to home, Sheerness-on-Sea.

Once I left home and moved around the country for study or work, visits became much less frequent, though I always retained my affection for the town. In fact, my parents long harboured the desire of retiring to Folkestone (on their last holiday together they had stayed in the Grand Burstin Hotel beside the harbour), but with my mother's relatively early passing, it never materialised. But their groundwork was not done in vain, as when the opportunity arose in 2016, my wife and I had no hesitation in moving here.

I have gathered together thirty three of my poems inspired by Folkestone, in which many of the themes and events I have outlined above are referenced and explored. One challenge has been whether to present them in a systematic way, for example, chronology, geography or subject matter, but ultimately, they are laid before you in an essentially random form, at least superficially.

Tony Quarrington
Folkestone
March 2023

When the Young Boy Arrived
(apologies to Philip Larkin)

Life was never better
Than in Nineteen Sixty Three
Between the end of the snowbound winter
And Freddie's *You Were Made For Me*.

On a cool August morning in Foord Road South,
A blue Vauxhall Victor groans to a stop,
Disgorging two pairs of flustered parents
And three children chock full of crisps and pop.

No sooner has the guest book been signed
The kids plead to go to East Cliff Sands;
With the tide far out the strand is ripe for
Sandcastles with flags and wonky handstands.

But it is cricket the boy yearns for the most,
Pitching stumps and bails he scans the beach
For willing, smaller boys to field for him
While he smashes the ball out of their reach.
As sand recedes beneath insistent waves,
Cricket gives way to crazy golf with slides,
To putting green and boating lake,
Rollercoasters and Rotunda rides.

He plays for plastic racing cars
And pinball machine high scores,
While parents play bingo for household goods
That could be bought cheaper in local stores.

And then there's that first trip abroad
On a ferry bound for Boulogne-Sur-Mer;
The boy spends his time bent overboard,
In tired tears and sad, silent prayer.

But he cheers at promise of fish and chips,
White bread and butter, man-size mug of tea;
And climbing the crooked, sloping street
To stare at *Rock Shop*'s window wide and free.

Life was never better
Than in Nineteen Sixty Three
Between the end of the snowbound winter
And Freddie's *You Were Made For Me*.

A Writer's Town

This is a writer's town.

Where, in quiet corners of coffee shops,
Caressing cake and cappuccino,
On new varnished cliff top benches,
In untidy, tiny studio apartments,
And above galleries and gift shops,
Diligently, they polish their craft
In solitude and patient struggle.

Where, down the steep, unforgiving hill,
Past higgledy-piggledy buildings
That shelter the secrets of centuries,
Old men, like modern day gunslingers,
Shuffle with shabby, sagging satchels
Stuffed with story scraps and post-it notes,
Lassoed around their wrinkled necks.

Where restless waves wash over shingle,
Shifting the site of a billion pebbles,
And where small, redundant, fishing boats,
Their hulls rotting and history forgotten,
Are nudged and tickled by the turning tide
And left for dead as the sea sweeps back.
Where, on a mile long thoroughfare
Of lawn and flowers and grand hotels,

Echoes of genteel, whispered discourse
Float across the unremitting breeze,
And the plaintive cry of a seagull chick
Resonates across the ragged rooftops.

Where the solemn chimes of an ancient church
Dedicated to an Anglo-Saxon girl,
Ring out at dusk under Shelley's pale moon,
And where cracked, crippling, stony steps
Unsettle the anxious wandering scribe
Searching seaward for that elusive line.

This is a writer's town.

Our Lady of the Harbour

No fey fairy figure this Folkestone maid
But mature, full-bodied, strong and wise,
Rooted firmly on the East Head rocks
Staring intently out on mottled skies.

Some try to clothe her in pity, some in fun -
Hats, scarves and masks have all adorned her form,
But she is perfect as she is - broad, naked, deep,
Impervious to pounding waves and winter storms.

Her hair forever drenched from tidal spray
Slicked back and sweeping down her spine;
Her lusty feet replace the mermaid's tail,
Resist and spurn the bitter lapping brine.

To the dogs released from summer servitude
On Sunny Sands she's just another stone
Their ball might bounce upon from owner's throw,
Or where they can relieve themselves alone.

Twelve summers has she now been settled there,
Yet it seems to have been so many more,
As if she'd witnessed history's changing tides,
Declining fish trade and the road to war.
When packet steam trains trundled down the hill
Into the harbour station and France bound ships,

When English tommy first tasted foreign food -
Snails, mussels, garlic, frites instead of chips.

I clamber across still slippery lower rocks
To reach the stone she's made her home,
And sit at her feet to see what *she* might see,
While thwarting tourists with their camera phones.

Could she be looking to Calais or Boulogne?
But rather her gaze looks upwards to the sky,
As if in thanks this piece of Heaven should be
Where Cornelia Parker chose that she should lie.

Oblivious to the sights and sounds around,
The squawk of seagulls or wave smashed shore,
Mindless of games that gleeful children play
Upon the drying beach when tide withdraws.

Margate may have its Turner, Blackpool its Tower,
Brighton its *i360*, St Ive's its *Tate*,
But none sing of the sea like our Folkestone girl,
Stately and brave at England's coastal gate.

I rise from the rocks with wet, creaking knees,
While hers are as fresh and smooth as first she came,
Two hours have passed since first I joined her there,
A better use of time I could never dare to claim.

Two ferries pass each other in Dover's strait
As the sun slides down into a silvery sea,
Over her shoulder through darkening clouds
The cliffs of France gleam and bid "bonne nuit".

Autumn Morning

The pre-dawn chorus of ducks
And gulls, jackdaws and crows,
And a single menacing magpie,
Puncture the sinister silence
Of a new Radnor Park day.

Untimely ripped from fractured slumber,
I prepare for my daily ritual
Of checking if the sea is still there,
And that my recent relocation
Is not a dream after all.

Caught in a feverish leaf storm
Along Castle Hill Avenue,
Joni in my ears telling me
She's seen life from both sides now,
I cross newly crowned Bouverie village
And traffic lined Sandgate Road.

And there it is –
That
Ever
Never
Changing view!
Dover and Dungeness
Take their early morning bows.

The dew-soaked Leas is rife with life -
Walkers, joggers, mobility scooters,
And teenagers with learning difficulties
On escorted pilgrimages around town.

Vacant, whispering benches
Call out across the century,
Reminders of courage and sacrifice
That allow me
To wallow in
This stunning spectacle today.

As an insipid sun appears,
Parched dogs yank at leads
And pause to lap the cool water
Filling the empty margarine boxes
Left outside the Leas Cliff Hall.

Setting Sail for France

From many centuries of slog and slime,
From Pent Stream and Channel battered,
A sleepy, careworn fishing village
Today becomes a town that matters.

Herring, mackerel, crabs and sole
Now make their way to Billingsgate,
And fetch a price not seen before
The railway raised flat Folkestone's fate.

Sun, with constant bedfellow, breeze,
Smiles on the sight of first class fares,
While locals rush to viewing points
From auction sheds where plied their wares.

First wave of "down from London" folk
Step from gleaming horse drawn coach
That brought them from a makeshift station
In lieu of new rail track approach.

A boisterous band blares out the latest hits
Of Wagner, Chopin, Strauss and Liszt,
As crinolined ladies, with handbags and fans,
Tease gentlemen whose advances they resist.

Steam powered *Water Witch*, focal point
Of this auspicious day, adjoins the quay,
And nervous passengers scramble aboard
In clothes unsuited for a swelling sea.

But the water's calm and the crossing smooth
As guns and flags bid travellers adieu;
In just three hours, on Boulogne's full dock,
An even louder sound greets guests and crew.

La Marsellaise and *God Save the Queen*
Salute the excited but exhausted crowd,
A solid sign of entente cordiale,
Two towns so far, but now so near, made proud.

In Folkestone, normal service is resumed,
Men mend nets and women cook and clean,
Habitual chores for a thousand years,
Yet a smaller, faster, world can now be seen.

The Old High Street Awakens

Cowboy boot heels on sodden cobbles,
Dalla Cortes steam in the freezing air,
The sloping street where art and cake
Have usurped beach balls, pottery and rock,
Imperceptibly slips into life.

A perilous pedestrian chicane
Of chalk advertising boards
Takes shape, promoting everything
From wholefoods, tapas and pizza,
Rude greeting cards and doggie treats
To vintage vinyl and local art,
Kidswear and Krishna consciousness.

Postman in worn, workaday shorts
And knobbly knees that rival mine,
Darts cheerfully from door to door,
While window cleaner leans his ladder
Against ledges of upstairs studios
Where artist residents sleep in late.

White van men pull up at Payers Park
And, sweating, stagger down the hill
To deliver kitchen rolls and clothing stock,
And polystyrene coffee cups,
Only to discover it is Monday
And most businesses are closed,
Except *Steep Street Coffee House*,
Now unofficial sorting office.

A triumvirate of weary sprucers,
Unheralded heroes of this dirty town,
Trudge past the *The Quarter Masters* store
Trailing bags of indeterminate bulk,
Culled from an early morning raid
On the *Party Bar* and Harbour Street.

A small curly haired toddler,
Dressed head to toe in Peppa Pig pink,
Skips gleefully down the street,
While her frantic father strains to
Grab her hand before she rolls
Towards a potentially watery grave.

Should he fail, however,
I am comforted that
Low tide is set to last a little longer.

I Sit in Coffee Shops

I sit in coffee shops.
That's what I do,
Sometimes outside
To take in the view.

There I write poems
Or post updates online,
To let my friends know
That I'm doing fine.

I might have a big breakfast,
Or occasionally brunch,
And if I stay long enough
It might stretch to lunch.

Cappuccino, no chocolate
Is my customary drink,
But after two or three
I can't hear myself think.

So I revert to a pot
Of refreshing Earl Grey,
Instead of just leaving
It allows me to stay.
I quite like the quiet
But am up for a natter,

With anyone else
There for that matter.

If I'm using my laptop
Which is not that robust,
To keep it performing
A wall socket's a must.

Django's and *Steep Street*
Are my favourite haunts,
Gourmet Kitchen and *Folklore*
And *Brew* on my jaunts.

I love the *Lift Cafe*
By the regeneration,
But miss *Bobbies* so
In the old harbour station.

Ken's *Hillside Café*
Is the daddy of them all,
Forty eight years and counting
It's answered the call.

I sit in coffee shops,
That's what I do,
Sometimes outside
To take in the view.

Sweet Pent Flow Softly

From Danton Farm to Folkestone's harbourside,
The watercourse winds down towards the sea;
Now largely hidden from the public gaze,
It still has the power to damage you and me.

Imprisoned in pipes by Channel Tunnel,
Passing through Morehall and Three Hills Park,
It weaves its way alongside new housing,
Appears and disappears at different marks.

Beside the metal footbridge at Broadmead
It resurfaces in Lower Radnor Park,
Where it glides and ambles beneath tall trees
That screen the glinting sun and pierce the dark.

Empty crisp packets and chocolate wrappers
Lie wedged among the stream stroked rocks,
Ivy draped grotto manifests neglect,
Moss stained stones and stagnant water mock.

But, vouchsafed by Victorian forebears,
It remains a quiet refuge from the race;
Where scurrying squirrels pursue their tails
And jackdaw and magpie compete for space.
Dog walkers tramp along the muddy track
That leads to paved Pavilion Road,

And one last glimpse of curved rivulet,
By fence at foot of *Red Cow* garden flowed.

No more source of fresh water for the town,
No more driving force for Foord Road mill,
No more home on planks for fishing folk,
Shoved underground a shopping need to fill.

From Tontine Street beneath the fountains,
It meets returning tide by harbour wall;
A quiet end perhaps, but still pent up threat
In times of storm and flood that may yet call.

Queueing for Potatoes

A day like any other -
In the middle of a war.

Except it isn't.

Anticipation swells as
Gertie and Mabel Bowbrick,
And doting mother, Nellie,
Wait patiently, cheerfully in line
Outside *Stokes* the greengrocers
On teeming Tontine Street,
For a special delivery of
Scarce fruit and vegetables
Later that warm spring afternoon.

At twenty minutes past six,
With glowering clouds
Concealing surprise,
What sounds like gunfire
Is heard from the direction of
Shorncliffe Army Camp.

"It's just training manoeuvres,
It happens all the time"
Is the general consensus
Among an indifferent crowd,

Reassured that Blighty
Remains up for the fight.

Until two minutes later,
When people and premises
Are laid low by single bomb,
Casually propelled from
Passing enemy planes.

Frederick and Arthur Stokes,
Their family and staff,
Perish on the spot,
Along with Gertie and Mabel,
Florrie and Willie Norris
And many more.

Sixty one slain in total,
Youngest three months old;
In Folkestone and elsewhere
Thirty six more lives snuffed out,
Before the final toll is known
Nearly eight years later,
When indomitable Nellie
Draws her last breath in the
Royal Victoria Hospital,
Half a mile from the scene.

No rationing of potatoes that day,
Rather a rationing of civilian lives
Lost in a line of innocence and hope.

Today, flanked by brewery tap
And greasy spoon,
A small, pale blue plaque,
Sometimes furnished
With a spray of flowers,
Stands before a neglected,
Bare, open patch of land,
Where tenacious weeds
Thrust through shards of slate.

Waiting for the Tide (A Gull's Life)

Beside *Bob*'s whitewashed stall,
With slogan "*Fresh seafood subject*
To sea conditions and hangovers",
A fearless chick loiters with intent,
Affecting to ignore the cartons of
Cockles and whelks and lobster tails
Dispensed a few short steps away,
But pouncing on any edible debris,
Unwittingly or deliberately dropped
By thoughtless human passers-by.

By Pent's red brick journey's end
They luxuriate in a bracing shower
In muddy, minute puddles left behind
By gone, at least for now, high water;
With half an eye in the direction
Of *Chummy's* charitable staff who
Fling empty shells onto a stony floor.

Teetering on bare, oarless rowing boats,
Or perched on piles of greying wood
Wedged deep into the thickening mud,
They pass the interminable time

Till small craft stir and sway again,
And the sun winks on wind-blown water.

An earnest, fretful throng assembles
At the end of *Rocksalt*'s sloping jetty,
Squabbling over the best viewing spot
To wait in line for the painfully slow
Returning tide to reappear;
In the meantime, scavenging for scraps
On Stade's cobbled, concrete floor,
Disdainfully discarding bottle tops,
Dog ends and paper coffee cups.

Shrieks and cries rise in intensity
As the prodigal, once truant, tide
Floods through Folkestone's golden gate
Between now closed off East Head
And war-remnants of South Quay.

A startled chick chases after its mother,
Emitting a constant stream of whistles,
Pleading for a morsel of the fresh fish
Now washing over its grateful feet;
But peevish parent pecks its bobbing head
And bids it bide its time for now.

Mermaid Beach at Dusk

On a night like this,
The Cote d'Opale
Might as well be
A thousand miles away.

Sea and sky present
An ashen canvas,
Impossible to tell
Where one ends
And the other begins.

Barely a whisper from the surf;
Even Arnold's
"Grating roar of pebbles"
Is indecipherable,
So faint is nature's refrain.

Across town,
Above an old post office,
A neon sign proclaims that
"Heaven is a place
Where nothing ever happens".

And nothing *is* happening tonight.

But then *everything* is happening.

The lighthouse blinks through
Thick, enfolding gloom;
A tuneless, forsaken church bell
Hangs silently suspended above
The empty beach where,
On earlier nights,
Hundreds might have revelled.

A cockapoo puppy snuffles among
Seaweed encrusted pebbles,
And ignores its owner's
Impassioned and fruitless pleas
To accompany her back to the
Refuge of her Range Rover
Parked at the foot of the desolate lift.

An empty tuna mayonnaise
Sandwich carton flutters
In the breathless breeze.

A lone fisherman plants tripod and rod
Beside the dark, deserted shore,
Reminding me of all night sessions
On otherworldly Dungeness beach
With my teddy boy "Uncle Len"
And Elvis and Buddy on the radio,
More than sixty years ago.

Tomorrow morning, life will return,
Fearless ladies of a certain age
Will tiptoe shivering beside stone groynes

Until they slip slowly into the glacial water,
When trepidation will
Give way to exhilaration,
Before craving the comfort
Of dry robes and towels
And sanctuary of new beach huts.

Coffee Shop Devotional

A soulful sixties hymnal
Greets the bevy of believers
Congregating
For morning service
In the brightly lit
Book-crammed cafe.

A quartet of young mothers,
Grappling with babies,
Buggies and baggage,
Claim the larger pews
On the upper floor
For their weekly convocation -
Tales of toddler tantrums
And reality television.

A solemn young couple,
Festooned in facial piercings
And many more beneath
Black, capacious vestments,
Extract laptops from rucksacks
And set silently to prayer on
Processing online orders for
Their goth fashion business.

On an adjacent table,
A pony-tailed interviewer and
Nervous but earnest candidate
Negotiate a sinecure in the
Creative Quarter team.

But all heads are suddenly turned
As a round glass cloche, containing
Lemon, almond and polenta cake
Is borne on high from the kitchen
To gasps and licking of lips,
And the communicants
Line up for their slice
And a caramel macchiato.

Out on Bayle

Welcome retreat from the rush of town,
Enough off the beaten track
To be sheltered from the multitude,
Lies a haven of civility and peace.

Beyond charming Church Street,
Past splintered, leaning lychgate
And ancient battered headstones,
Each, from their frail condition,
Seeming drunk on communion wine,
The magnificent mediaeval church
Cuts a benevolent figure
As it oversees the proud village.

Fourteen centuries since
She walked these quiet streets,
The spirit of an Anglo-Saxon girl
Of royal blood and fervent piety
Still permeates the atmosphere,
Her bones, for so long concealed,
Now a serious site for pilgrimage.

Neat pastel hued houses
And weatherboarded cottages
Cohabit in engaging harmony;
Even the modern apartment block
Blends unobtrusively.

Bayle Pond Gardens,
Once brimful with water
Conjured uphill from Guildhall Street
By Eanswythe for her nunnery,
Later inhabited by gliding swans,
Is now home to art by
Patrick Corillon and Tracey Emin
And a dazzling display of flowers.

Historic hostelries stand sentry
At either end of the main street,
One the oldest watering hole in town
And erstwhile local of
Mr Dickens from Albion Villas,
The other, welcoming second home
To men stationed at adjoining garrison.

Atop heart pounding Parade steps
Stands mysterious and magical
Shangri-La, discredited as
Enemy spy hole in time of war,
(The poet ducks for cover),
But still with incomparable views
Over the harbour towards France.

A few steps away a small garden,
Skilfully conceived and lovingly tended,
Acts as the embodiment of
A community whose spirit burns bright.

Like the memory of that young girl
In simpler times so long ago.

A Grand Opening

Perambulators and parasols parade
On newly mown and manicured lawn
Designed by Decimus Burton,
From polo field and pasture hewn.

"Finest marine promenade in the world",
The guidebook effusively lays claim;
Hard to argue on this glorious morn
When sea and sky look just the same.

The guests arrive by lift and carriage,
Depending on their wealth and style,
To acclaim a marvel of the modern age,
A red brick vision to raise a smile.

Crowds congregate on Madeira Walk,
Path forged from latest cliff landslide,
While builder Baker, spurned by *Metropole*,
Admires his handiwork with rightful pride.

The band plays a medley of popular tunes,
From jazz, music hall and ragtime,
Like *When We Were Two Little Boys*,
And *In the Good Old Summertime.*
Albert Burvill, in new blue uniform,
Sends packing gatecrashers from town

Craving a peek at the rich folk's party,
Now turned away by copper's frown.

But they will get their chance another day
To press their noses to the "Monkey Cage",
And watch their King among his court
Feast and roar on this most public stage.

Metropole management looks on
At rival Radnor vowed never to build,
Contemplating legal action
Against violation of its private field.

Pavilion, *Burlington*, *Majestic*,
Metropole and now the *Grand*,
Fashionable Folkestone is all the rage
By harbour and on cliff top land.

A Path Fit for Heroes

For Folkestone's servicemen
Denied the promised gift of work
On their return from war in France,
One landmark stands testimony
To their press-ganged endeavour.

The Zig Zag Path twists and turns,
At times gently, at others steeply,
From cliff top bandstand
To seafront's edge,
A new and spectacular view
At every necessary pause for breath.

Built from a creative cocktail
Of rocks and bricks, rubble and sand,
Softened by trees and flower beds,
Its tunnels, caves and arches
A less strenuous route
Than those *"breakneck flights
Of ragged steps"* that
Dickens warned against.

As I scan the scene
From Mermaid Beach,
Through the Amphitheatre frame,
With sun shining overhead,
I might almost be in Santorini;

All that is missing, mercifully,
Are the mangy, maltreated mules
And their mountain of excrement.
Tonight, in a dank, dark, grimy grotto,
Girls giggle at boys' fumbling foreplay
Fuelled by cannabis and cheap cider.

As the path turns one hundred years
Since it was first unveiled,
Can these be our modern day heroes?

Dust in my Cappuccino

Concrete and cranes now bestride the beach
Between Marine Parade and coastal park,
Steel scaffolding scars and scrapes the skyline;
The howls of herring gulls and lapping waves,
Reassuring melodies of the seafront scene,
Are now drowned by the discordant notes
Of drill and digger, hammer and saw.

Switchback, swimming pool and pier,
Putting, boating lake and llama rides,
Once the beating heart of local life,
All now just melancholy memories,
Mourned on social media platforms.

In their place, behind the boardwalk,
That separates the sea and building site,
A new, brighter world is taking shape
On shell and shifting shingle land.

Deteriorating old lift cars
Lie side by side in sad neglect,
Trapped halfway up the disused track,
Impatient for the new flats to rise
And hasten their own resurrection.

I loiter outside the former waiting room,
Now popular pitstop on the promenade
For builders, cyclists and curious tourists,
With a vegan sausage roll in my hand

And dust in my cappuccino.

Where Old Ghosts Meet

I

A biting breeze and thin drizzle
Denote December's inevitable
If uninvited return;
Twilight descends
On the ancient churchyard.

Never has the phrase
"Quiet as the grave"
Seemed more apt.

As I pause to tie my bootlaces
By the Town Cross, venue for
Mayor making for centuries,
My body shudders as
A young woman brushes past,
The hem of her blue dress
Grazing the grass border,
And her white headpiece
Fluttering in the wind.

She carries provisions -
Bread, leeks and a
Small flagon of beer -
For the poor of the parish

In a round wicker basket,
Forswearing another
Potentially lucrative tryst
With a Northumbrian nobleman,
Orchestrated by a desperate father.

Her head bowed, she whispers
"Good evening, sir, God be with you".
Before I can frame
An intelligible response,
She disappears behind the west window.

Composing myself as best I can,
I shamble past unremembered tombs,
Narrowly avoiding a collision
With a rat scuttling across my path
To the comparative sanctuary
Of the lopsided lychgate
Leading into Church Street.

The *Pullman* pub is empty,
Save for a few flickering candles
And a lone member of bar staff
Interrogating his mobile phone.

The lanterns of Rendezvous Street,
Pride of Victorian town planners,
Glimmer dimly, and the restaurants
Are sparsely populated.

The stillness is unnerving
But strangely thrilling.

II

I enter the narrow, twisting,
Rain drenched street that
Slides down towards the harbour.

Many months have elapsed since
Chaotic, cacophonous *Charivari*
Had snaked up that old thoroughfare,
All drums and whistles and cymbals
And less conventional instruments.

More recently, the ground had groaned
Beneath the bullish burden of
Polished, red-laced *"Doc" Martens*,
Worn by follicly challenged pilgrims
Strutting towards *The Ship* and *Royal George*
For an afternoon of *Special Brew*
And worship at the altar of
Prince Buster and *The Specials*.

I am alone.

But am I?

The fog in my brain mirrors
The slowly enveloping mist
Swirling around the foot of the hill;
Fragmented images of times past
In this salty, saintly seaside town
Overwhelm my thoughts.

Nothing is quite what it seems.

My longing for one last lingering look
At the dazzling daily alchemy
Conjured up in *Rowland's* rock shop
Is soon dramatically answered.

The heady, fashionable aromas of
Craft beer and Nicaraguan coffee
Cannot compete with the memory
Of the sickly sweet perfume
Radiating from that beloved spot
Where, nose squashed against the glass,
A small boy gasped at the
Long sticks of heaven being rolled.

"Let me in at the front, Michael,
You've been stood there for ages",
Pleads his tearful younger sister, Anna,
Her view obscured by the taller girl
Planted thoughtlessly in front of her.

"Have they started giving out the bags
Of broken bits yet?", another boy
Bellows from further back in the crowd.

A sudden, excited scrum confirms
His suspicion as I catch an
Intoxicating whiff of granulated sugar.

It was often claimed that if *Rowlands*
Were to shut its doors for good,
Folkestone would die - a prediction,
Since proven thankfully
And conclusively
Wrong.

III

I pass by *Marley's* - or what
I think is *Marley's;*
From a dark upstairs room,
Redolent of patchouli
And "cigarette" smoke,
A loud, throbbing jukebox
Exhorts me to
 "Go to San Francisco" ,
A seductive reminder
Of the *Summer of Love*
On a bleak winter's evening.

Two young men in afghan coats
And a messy profusion of facial hair,
Are huddled half way up
The sheer, crumbling Bayle Steps.

"Hey man, how's it goin'?"

"Far out, whatcha doin' tonight?"

"Goin' to Archies. The Lonely Ones are playing".

"Nice. I hear there's some hot Swedish chicks in town too".

"That's settled then, Archie's it is".

"Yeah, and I could kill for one of his salami rolls right now".

I start to follow them through the door,
Only to discover that the closer I get,
The scene dissolves and I am

Left once more outside
Marley's rather than the *Acropolis*.

IV

The nipping cold slices through my
Flimsy denim jacket as I try to
Rationalise the events of
The past half an hour.

I cross a deserted Tram Road car park
And pass under the arch by *Ovenden's*
Forge into the empty fish market,
Tiptoeing around the putrid puddles
That tend to settle there,
Whether it has rained or not.

A solitary gull plods apologetically past,
Pining for Spring and the reopening of
Chummy's and *Bob's* seafood stalls,
When it will again be afforded means,
Motive and opportunity to ambush tourists
For fish and chips and tubs of whelks.

Pausing outside *The Shell Shop* I watch
Men in cloth caps and mud caked boots
Tramp up the slipway opposite, lobster pots
And herring nets half empty after
An exhausting and disheartening shift.
They slap their meagre catch
On the floor of *Fish Shed One*,

Light *Woodbine* and *Senior Service* cigarettes
And gather in whispered conversation.
'Darkie" Fagg, "Cottage" Featherbe
And "Lobby" Spearpoint lean on the railing
And reminisce about better days,
While "Old Ned" Saunders,
Retired these ten years,
Mends sprat and mackerel nets
For a "free" pint or two in
The *Oddfellows Arms* this evening.

On The Stade, wives and daughters
Juggle the demanding tasks of
Cleaning fish and supervising the
Younger and not so fragrant children.

It is difficult to determine
Which gender has it tougher.

Meanwhile, grubby, barefoot young boys,
Oblivious to the dedication and drudgery
Of their elders around them,
Chalk stumps on the wall of *Clouts Alley*.

"I'll be Jack "Obbs, you can be Clarrie Grimmett.
I'll 'it you into the "arbour, every time, just you see"
Brags nine year old Harry Sharp.

But with his first delivery, Clarrie,
Better known about these parts as Edmund,
And, in later years, "La La", Taylor,

Traps Jack in front of his wicket
And appeals for leg before.

"Owzat! Got you with me flipper, pom".

A heated dispute ensues, culminating in
The great English batsman hurling his bat
Against the wall and storming off
In the direction of *Redman's* boat builders.

His mother, ankle deep in half gutted dogfish
And three scruffy toddlers, calls:

"'Arry, your tea is ready;
And find your blinkin' brother
Before you come in".

"Five more minutes, mum. I've got to bowl
Don Bradman out first, it won't take long".

"Five more minutes, my arse -
You've got thirty seconds,
This tea won't wait.
If you don't get to the table soon,
The other kids will have your share".

A case of bad mum stopped play.

V

As this scene of family harmony evaporates,
I hear, from across the harbour,
Behind the *Royal Pavilion Hotel*,
A sergeant major's earsplitting admonition
To *"Step Short"* to a long procession

Of uniformed men striding down
The slope from the Leas above.

The rhythmic sound of boots
On concrete is accompanied by
Raucous renditions of "*Pack up
Your Troubles In Your Old Kit Bag*"
And "*It's a Long Way to Tipperary*",
As the soldiers march to waiting ships
And likely death on the Western Front.

But there is one last treat
Before their sombre adventure begins.

Inside the harbour station waiting room,
Two formidable middle aged women
Adjust their pinafores and rearrange
Any curls that have slipped beneath
Their flower bestrewn boaters
And inspect the massive urns
Containing the last hot, strong tea
Most of these men will ever drink.

"*Come on boys, form a straight line,
You don't have long, you know*",
Flora Jeffrey cries with a tinge of regret
In her voice, while her sister Margaret
Cuts thin slices of trench cake
And bread pudding.

"*And don't forget to sign the visitors' book
Before you do*".

"*All right, you sound like me muvver -
Nag, nag, nag*", one private who claims

To be twenty one but looks sixteen,
Retorts, as he lurches towards Flora
And slurs:

"Gizza kiss".

But before he can perfect this unwise manoeuvre,
A grizzled veteran of Ladysmith and Mafeking
Yanks him back by his collar and barks:

"Show the ladies some respect, young 'un'.
You ain't in the playground now, y'know".

"Sorry, old timer, I didn't mean nuffin'
By it, it was just a bit of fun".

Flora chuckles: *"You got off lightly there,*
My boy, that's nothing to what
Margaret would have done
To you if you'd got any nearer!"

An outpouring of communal hilarity
Is unleashed, and the embarrassed teenager
Slinks back into the anonymity of the crowd.

VI

I leave the exuberant
But fearful throng
With the final strains of
"Keep the Home Fires Burning"
Ringing in my ears, and join

The boardwalk linking station
And sleeping water lift.

But I have hardly stepped foot
On the old railway sleepers
Before I find myself amidst
A jumbled assortment of buildings -
Swimming pool, boating lake
And fairground rides.

As I try to take all this in,
A crew cut kid in knitted cardigan
And khaki shorts is rushing
Into a huge, dimpled dome,
Destined to be his whole world
For the next two weeks;
He will never tire of rolling a penny
For plastic motor cars or shooting
A steel ball into a hole
For packets of mints.

His father and mother, the latter
Clutching a wad of paper tickets,
Frown as they dismount from the
Uncomfortable looking seats
They have occupied
For the past two hours,
Where they had been subjected to
An annoying loop of "*Legs eleven*",
"*Two little ducks, twenty two*",
Not to mention the collective snigger
That greets "*six and nine, sixty nine*".

The boy prises himself
From the penny pusher

And scampers towards them
In a frenzy of excitement.

"How many wins did you get, mum?".

"Eight".

His heart sinks.
*"Oh no, that wooden train set
On the bottom shelf is nine wins;
Can you play some more games
And win it for me?"*

*"We don't have time, darling;
Besides dad and I want that
Nice set of tea trays which
Will be just perfect for our
TV dinners when we get home".*

"Boring".

Feeling betrayed and despondent,
The boy skulks off in the direction of
The Runaway Coaster.

But he is soon appeased by
A promise of fish and chips
In his favourite restaurant
In Tontine Street.

VII

Intermittent sea fret has given way

To steady rain and a thickening gloom;
Hungry and shivering,
I resolve to return home.

Christmas lights decorate the street
As retailers and restaurant owners
Contend for the seasonal accolade
Of best dressed window,
Though tonight there is
Nobody about to judge them.

Silence is restored.

Until I reach *Archie's*.

Through that same shadowy upstairs window
From whence the Flowerpot Men
Had serenaded me two hours -
Or is it a hundred years - earlier,
The Small Faces remind me that:

"It's all too beautiful".

After the battering my senses have taken
This evening, I remain to be convinced
Of the veracity of this hypothesis.

So I try, for the second time,
To gain access to the old haunt
Of hippies and hedonists.

I take my first hesitant steps,
Expecting to land in *Marley's* again,

The doors open of their own accord

And I am permitted to enter.

And there, waiting to greet me,
Is the genial owner, Mickey Argegrou,
Anxious to introduce me to his
Special guests for the night.

Astonishingly, St Eanswythe is here,
The modest blue and white garments
Worn during our perfunctory encounter
In the churchyard earlier have been
Replaced by brightly coloured, patterned
Flower dress, matching newsboy hat
And knee length white plastic boots.

She is sampling her first cup of coffee
And, judging by the uncharacteristic grimace
That follows a single sip, she is unlikely
To order a second, water from her own spring
And the occasional small goblet of mead,
Will remain her preferred tipples.

With the final troop ship of the day, *Engadine,*
Set sail for Boulogne, and the *Mole Cafe*
Consequently closed,
The indomitable Jeffrey sisters have swapped
Pinafores for elegant cocktail dresses;
They appear to be conducting a taste test
Of Mickey's famed rum babas,
Comparing them in the process
To their revered fruit cake.

John Brickell, still in his overalls
And safety cap, is here too,
Disappointing his adoring army of young fans

By holding back the rock shop remnants,
Instead distributing them to
The grateful regulars
As a perfect accompaniment
To their drinks.

And Harry Sharp, grown in the past hour
Into a handsome young man,
But still smarting from his first ball duck
At the Clouts Alley Oval,
Is feeding the jukebox,
While Old Ned Saunders, for the evening
Released from net repairing duties,
Though not separated from
His threadbare fisherman's jumper,
Is leading a communal singsong
To the latest tune selected by Harry:

"Those were the days, my friend".

Following the scenes
I have witnessed this evening,
I am inclined to agree.

East Cliff

In every tuft of dew-drenched grass
And every slice of crumbling chalk,
The howl of history is heard
Across this patch of green I walk.

Ferries no longer line the pier,
Nor steam from up trains fills the air,
The view replaced by Folkestone sign
And *Burstin*'s monumental glare.

Mouldering Martello tower,
Former lookout for all that floats,
Stares out today at pitch and putt
And bowling club instead of boats.

Above sharp pointed Peter's spire
The roar of spitfires still turns heads
Of tourists, swimmers, fishermen
And foragers on fossil beds.

The *Chinese Elvis* lives here now,
From Old Kent Road to East Wear Bay,
No ghetto or jailhouse in sight,
But bungalows and children's play.

On ten thousand year old *Jock's Pitch*,
Where breathless dogs now chase balls,
A caldarium bubbles underneath
And another chunk of cliff top falls.

The Seagull's Breakfast

Seagull, seagull sitting on a roof,
Seagull, seagull, resting and aloof.

No care in the world, so it would seem,
Silent and still, as if in a dream.

Meanwhile, in the cafe down below,
A full English breakfast is now on show.

In fifteen minutes, the plate is clean,
Save for a rasher and ten baked beans.

The customer pays and walks away
While the seagull contemplates its prey.

Before the server can clear the table first,
The seagull has swiftly done his worst.

Cutlery and crockery loudly clatter
While seats and tables ketchup splatter.

Bacon and beans gripped in his beak,
The gull retreats with triumphant shriek.

Soon peace and quiet return to the scene,
An Eggs Royale is ordered, all is serene.

But............

Seagull, seagull sitting on a roof,
Seagull, seagull, resting and aloof.

Triennial

Every three years, or sometimes four,
Art scholars and enthusiasts,
And others just plain curious,
Descend on Folkestone's streets
To gauge what all the fuss is about
In broadsheet newspapers
And stylish lifestyle magazines.

From late July's long, lazy afternoons
To the threshold of winter's chilling pall,
This self-styled *"gallery without walls"*
Has the wider art world in its thrall.

From Bradstone Road to Guildhall Street,
Kingsnorth Gardens to Bouverie Square,
They spill out from central railway station
And small, overburdened car parks,
Clutching brochures and *Google Maps*
Forever open on their smartphones.

Even forgotten and unfashionable
St Michael's Alley and Bournemouth Road
Have now joined Harbour, Leas and Bayle
For close attention on the tourist trail.

Artworks, symbols of a reimagined town,
Embellish our streets and promenades,
Creating honorary residents of
Boltanski, Hamid, Begum, and Bergman,
Wallinger, Ewan and Richard Woods.

It has its critics, it must be said,
Those who scream,
With a lack of understanding,
"A waste of taxpayers' money",
Those who, bizarrely, claim
"There is too much colour",
And then those aficionados
Who just dismiss it as a
"Load of old rubbish".

So, is it the foremost illustration
Of a once ailing town's rebirth?
A three month long indulgence
Of the creative cognoscenti
Closeted in a few small streets?
Or proof of a divided community
Where apathy and ignorance rule?
No doubt, it is an acquired taste,
But is this not the role of art,
To question, to surprise, to thrill,
To generate debate?

Three more years we now must wait
Before we get another shot,
When new art will adorn the town,
And Folkestone once again runs hot.

Checkpoint George

Six feet but two worlds apart,
But no border guards here,
No passport, negative Covid test
Or quarantine on leaving needed.

Down the gently curving street,
Where cattle once were led to slaughter,
Now home to hairdressers and hip cafes,
Reside two celebrated dining spots
Of wildly varied vintage and appeal.

A calm if confusing truce exists;
Tourists and creatives discuss
Visits to the Harbour Arm and
New Triennial collection,
Or merely salivate over their
Pornstar martinis.

While Ken, in grease stained
Red and white striped apron,
Patrols his venerable kingdom;
His grizzled regulars, relocated
From former station next door,

Now trendy tea tasting store,
Shuffle uneasily in the alley,
Their language no longer as fruity
As the chocolate strawberries
On display across the thin divide.

Choose your poison if you're passing -
Sausage and black pudding roll
Or cheese and ham croissant,
Builder's or matcha latte green tea,
Banana split or Belgian waffles.
All equally enticing it seems,
But few cross this virtual battlefield.

Along the narrow, grimy lane,
Past the site where once
Folkestone's first post box stood,
A drowsy border collie
Lies stretched out across
No man's land.

Breakfast at Marley's

"We *love local*", the menu discreetly declares,
And be it full English, vegan, porridge or toast,
There's no other brunch venue in town compares,
The fresh food and welcome make this no idle boast.

Hallowed hippie hangout half a century before,
Deafening juke box blasting in Archie's coffee bar,
Reefer smoke swirling round the dim, upper floor;
Then the *Acropolis*, now Folkestone's dining star.

My name quaintly spelt out in wooden Scrabble tiles
Beckons me to my accustomed window seat;
I sip my cappuccino while returning passing smiles,
No better spot from which to watch the winding street.

Among the mounted shelves and dried hops tree lights glint,
Local art and thank you cards furnish grey green walls;
I settle down to inspect my current poem print
And order food before the lunchtime menu calls.

My Kentish sausage breakfast bap arrives in time,
Two poached eggs sharing king sized sourdough bed;

To not eat every single scrap would be a crime,
Or of pomegranate seed salad leave a shred.
But how do I contrive to eat this luscious beast
While maintaining my natural elegance and poise?
Here the humble breakfast is a flavoursome feast;
I look down again upon the street towards *Big Boys*.

Strange how the enduring romance of the scene outside
Recedes when rain stained stone slabs no longer glisten,
But sitting here alone in the corner by this window,
Between the houseplants to cultured chat I listen.

Sunday on the Harbour Arm

This is where east meets west,
Sidney Street and Augusta Gardens;
Where London day trippers
Mix with Folkestone natives,
Hostilities suspended for an afternoon.

Tram Road traffic crawls and curls
Around a heaving Harbour Street,
Affording passengers a protracted view
Of much loved
And loathed
Grand Burstin.

A stiff breeze cools the searing sun
And sweeps champagne flutes
To a sudden and watery demise
In the spray that laps the lighthouse,
Proof that, sometimes, weather
Can be a first to place and time.

As the crowds assemble and
Place orders from their seats
In the old Goods Yard
For *Sole Kitchen* and *Big Blue Bus*,
Barney and the Pizza,
Il Pakerro and *Burrito Buoy*,

Live music has too returned
After long Covid induced absence.

Premier League football
Plays on the Harbour Screen
While station platforms,
Restored to former glory,
And new marketplace stalls,
Showcase local creativity
And entrepreneurial verve.

Beneath their feet
An iron man stands,
Disinterested,
Appearing and disappearing
With the changing tide.

Palm trees by pebbles at the *Pilot Bar*
Alongside *Rocksalt's* younger sister
Reinforce the tropical atmosphere,
Tempered by "cool" but cramped seating
In waltzers and deckchairs
As a nostalgic nod to former times.

In the morning, normal service will be resumed;
Out of towners will return
To Tower Hamlets, Hackney,
Hoxton, Bow and Bethnal Green
With plans for relocation next year.

And the Arm will be handed back
To anglers, seagulls and a few
Unsuspecting, dreaming souls
Drenched by crashing waves
Cascading over Tuttofuoco's sign.

But is this the lull before the storm?
Eden before the Fall?
Will those blissful views
Of wild, weird Warren and
Windswept, green East Cliff
Be there to thrill us still
In five, ten or twenty years,
Or will the thunder of pick and drill
Drown out those of bass and drum?

Conversation with a Seagull

As I step away from *Bob's* counter,
Freshly caught crab sandwich
Clutched firmly in my hand
For fear of avian ambush,
I am joined by an adult gull -
We will call him "Sid" -
(Because he is no ordinary gull
As we shall soon discover),
Who plants himself
At a respectful distance
Professing no interest in the
Half eaten fish and chips
Lounging seductively, dangerously
On the adjoining table.

As I take my first bite,
He does that endearing seagull trick
Of pretending to avert his eyes,
Whilst slyly tracking the course
My succulent sandwich takes
Between my hand and mouth.
A staring contest ensues,
I for one not daring to take my eyes off
My inscrutable guest for one second.

I try to rationalise with Sid:

"Feeding you is not good for you,
In fact it's cruel;
You will get ill if you
Persist in eating human food".

After shooing off an interloping chick,
He replies:

"Crab is hardly human food,
I've been eating it for years
And it's never done me any harm".

Taken aback by this surprising development,
I take another, more censorious, tack:

"But you ransack our waste bins
And leave the contents strewn everywhere".

Sid is unimpressed, and
After a surreptitious
But unprofitable
Lunge at my sandwich,
Exclaims:

"Well, that's down to you
Not putting your bins out properly;
We wouldn't take the food if it
Was securely tied and hidden away,
We can't be blamed for
Your slapdash behaviour".

Irritated that he appeared to
Have an answer for everything,
I resolve to play the excreta card -
That had to be the clincher:

"You have an unfortunate propensity"
(I had decided by now that
He was an educated sort of chap
And would understand such long words),
"For shitting everywhere too,
On our windows, our cars,
And even our kids, at times".

Sid took particular umbrage at this slur:

"Well, on that point, don't you humans
Claim that it is lucky?
So I can't fathom your problem here;
And we're only doing what comes naturally,
We've been doing it for thirty million years.

And another thing:

If you didn't leave so much
Of your crap like pizza and chips lying around,
Our evacuations might not be
As copious or disagreeable".

And before I have time to respond,
He tilts his head and
Turns on the full charm offensive
By adding:

"But come on, admit it,
When it comes down to it,
We are cute,
Aren't we?"

To Sit and Stare

"What is this life if full of care
We have no time to stand and stare?"
Davies's century old quote
Is as relevant today
As it was then.

But sitting works just as well.

And where better to do that
Than on a wooden bench
Atop the cliffs in the fresh air
Of England's garden coast?

But, I hear you ask:
"What has sitting on a bench
Ever done for us?"

Let me count the ways.

To "rest our legs".

To pause and breathe.

To think or meditate.

To eat lunch.

To read a book or newspaper
(Ok, or a tablet/phone).

To admire the view (and what a view!).

To watch the world go by.

To "people watch".

To "sunbathe".

To escape from conflict (at work or at home).

To grieve over disappointment or heartache.

To explore first love.

Or a combination of any of the above.

And then there are less conventional reasons:

To drink or take drugs.

To "hide" with a lover.

Every bench decorated with a plaque
That grieving families have had affixed

To commemorate the lives of
Lost, lamented loved ones.

A more life-affirming tribute
Than concrete crematorium slab.

A visible and practical reminder of
A calmer age in a feverish world,
Celebratory and consolatory
In equal measure.

So take whatever opportunity you can
To *"sit and stare"*.

You might finish that book.

Or at least your lunch.

On Sandgate Beachfront

On a bracing late spring day,
I spot a vacant, varnished bench
On Granville Parade's broad pathway,
And lay claim to exclusive occupancy
As morning flows into afternoon.

A slender strip of undulating stone beach
Stretches for miles in either direction,
A dazzling expanse of sea before it;
Dymchurch, Dungeness and Hythe
Hover beneath a shimmering heat haze.

Gently lapping waves and crunching shingle
Provide an age old, soothing soundtrack,
Until a family of raucous, ravenous gulls
Play out an episode of *Jeremy Kyle,*
*(*Or *Jerry Springer* for my American readers)
For a baffled but fascinated audience.

A sprinkling of kayakers, welcomed back
From lockdown driven banishment,
Hug the shoreline, neatly sidestepping
The visiting grey seal and cormorant
That have taken temporary residence.

Children clamber cautiously but eagerly
Among spray splashed rock groynes,
As shivering parents shelter behind
Rainbow striped windbreakers
And swig from cans of *Budweiser*.

Dogs, their owners, cyclists and buggies -
And slightly flustered pedestrians -
Dance an inelegant quadrille
As they contend for space
On the congested promenade,
Passing quaint coastguard cottages,
And the house where Hattie
First researched her role as matron.

Beach Cottage, from where Wells
Fought off flying shrimp at supper time
And shot at bottles with Joseph Conrad,
Stands loud and green at parade end
As the footpath narrows
Towards Big Brother Folkestone.

King Henry's castle, built and rebuilt
To thwart feared but never executed
Waves of French attack,
Nearly three hundred years apart,
Sits quiet, unconquered
And closed.

The Boat House cafe does brisk business
With coffee, ice cream, hotdogs and rolls;
Its complement of beachside furniture,
Boasting its signature features of

Flower vase and painted pebbles,
Welcomes a steady stream of customers.

Its former social distancing sign that read
"Stand back while I disinfect the railing",
Now a distant memory.

Sunscreen for the Apocalypse

Walking on the Leas has the same appeal
As ever it did when Alice Keppel strolled
Its green sward with her philandering king;
But this morning, there's an unfamiliar feel,
The world has changed, grown frail, dull and cold,
Though the blue sky screams out the start of Spring.

The peace along the path seems so surreal,
People keeping their distance, young and old,
As waves crash beneath and the small birds sing;
Nature mocks mankind's weak attempts to heal,
Bright sunshine sends the wind and rain on hold,
Our latest disobedience our last fling.

Enjoy the sun, stay out as long as you can,
You may get ill, but you may also get a tan.

Lake Life

With resident white mallard
On a seasonal sabbatical,
A newly arrived black cormorant
Struts and preens on the central isle
Of once named *Peter Pan's Pool*,
While ravenous pigeons wrestle
Over scarce, illicit bread stocks.

No more anglers cast silent floats
On teeming duck infested waters;
No rods and bait filled baskets
Clutter the narrow concrete path,
Forcing me to wade through
The muddied grassy verge
Disturbing a greedy gull
Stamping feet to tease tender worms.

A late arriving sun shines sheepishly
Above the mock Tudor tea rooms;
Nurses from minor injury unit
Snatch fag breaks on the corner
Where discarded dog ends,
And twigs from overhanging trees,
Entice the ducks into mistaking
Them for a scrumptious breakfast,
(The fags and twigs, not the nurses).

After a day when few people pass
To witness the birdlife bedlam,
Dusk descends on a noiseless scene,
And a serene moon rises high
Over Cheriton Road rooftops.

In the littered concrete shelter,
Where youths habitually congregate
To drink and smoke and lark about
To heaving boombox accompaniment,
There is neither light nor sound -
No need for enforced curfew here.

Abandoned Harbour

Even the gulls are taking a morning off
As I drift around the desolate harbour;
The tide is out, the sky deep blue,
And the beach warm and yielding
Under my inappropriate footwear.

Amidst this light brown desert,
Thin streams of muddy water
Command me to take a hop,
Skip and jump to reach the
Next patch of solid dry sand.

Railway viaduct now fenced off,
Grand Burstin and *Rocksalt*
Both dark and sad and empty;
And the metal gates to the Harbour Arm,
Planned venue for thousands
On this warm Easter weekend,
Are firmly shut.

Though, along the walkway,
"Gormley" still manages a wink
At the doughty mermaid
On dog-filled Sunny Sands;
Cormorants, gulls and a solitary jogger
Usurp the space where tables and

Chairs for champagne drinkers
Might, in another time,
Have been spread out.

On a morning as beautiful as this,
It would have been perfect
To stroll its two concrete tiers;
But the only tears today
Are for the sick and fearful
Confined to home and hospital
Across an anxious land.

A pair of deep wrinkled fishermen
Lean against the chain railing
And reminisce
When fish were plentiful,
The ferries full
And fear a forgotten emotion.

I bound another murky stream
And lean against a fake pink house;
Planted in self-isolation,
Its former lustre lost too,
With peeling paintwork, and ponder
The fate of the next Triennial,
Triumphantly, but now pointlessly,
Announced a month -
But another lifetime - ago.

I turn the corner of the East Head
Under the rock perched orange house,
With its reviving lick of paint;

Two young girls lift their skirts,
And paddle in the shallow waves
On the incessant, incoming tide;
I cannot avoid the uncharitable suspicion that,
A sign of these strange and fretful times,
As they giggle and jostle each other,
They may not be from the same household.

Across the Muddied Park

Across the muddied park you lie there still,
Not stirring since we fell into this trance,
Inanimate, yet always on the move
For those few valued folk who have the chance.

More than a year now since last we made
That short train trip together into town,
But now as I slide by your door each day,
All I feel is your unintended frown.

I cannot resist a short, sideways glance
To validate that you still wait for me,
Longing for the day we can reconnect
And take that journey once again carefree.

I know I can still stroke your icy hands
Along the wall that leads to freedom's gate,
But it is there that I must stop and stare,
In twin fear and hope for our present state.

Across the muddied park you lie there still,
Not stirring since we fell into this trance,
Inanimate, yet always on the move
For those few valued folk who have the chance.

The Sea Pavilion (Casa Anacaona)

Sounds of a fiddle, lute and two guitars
And four rich, rousing, rusty voices,
Soar across the shell and shingle
Of a Kentish beach at twilight.

Songs of shipwrecks and drowning sailors,
Of girls waiting on an English shore
For their lovers of a single night,
Never more to lie in each other's arms;
Melancholy maritime melodies meet
The Venezuelan vivacity of this venue.

There is comedy too
As the audience grapples with
Frayed, salvaged deckchairs which,
Despite the march of technology
Over the past six decades,
Continue to confound the wit
Of the average Englishman.

But these are minor irritations,
Gleefully and stoically endured
For the healing thrill of live music
Beneath a beaming moon again.

Burstin' Back into Life

Waves sweep through railway arches
And *Rip Tide* and *Isabella,*
Sea Warrior and *Connemara,*
Long time inner basin residents,
Swing and sway
To a soaring seagull symphony.

Folkestone's *Marmite* building too
Comes to life once more;
Buses from Runcorn, Rhyl and Redcar
Offload oversized congregations,
Suitcases outnumbered by
Disability impedimenta.

The quayside is converted
From pedestrian thoroughfare
To geriatric racetrack
As mobility scooters
Scatter unwary walkers,
While rickety zimmer frames
Clog up the wide, windowed doorway.
An elderly couple from Cleckheaton,
Weary and windswept from seafront stroll,
Stagger from harbour fish bar
To plant their tired torsos
On the refuge of roadside benches.

Weekend specials are back on the menu,
With almost every still standing Sixties star
Scheduled to perform in the coming months.

Inside, there's not a spare seat
In the suffocating heat of the lounge bar;
Tables are laden with leftover sandwiches
And half empty glasses of gassy beer;
Debate lurches from Covid controls
To rabid rants about refugees,
Inflamed by hate-filed headlines
In the crumpled copies of the
Daily Mail and *Daily Express*
Left lying on abandoned chairs.

Another bus, bound for Margate,
Sandwich, Canterbury or Chatham,
Parks outside to await the sedentary rush
From couch to coach in thirty seconds;
Its passengers forsaking Folkestone
No sooner than they have arrived,
Only to return to eat and sleep tonight
Before escaping again to towns
No more deserving of their patronage.
Dover Docks and Cap Gris-Nez
Lurk somewhere beyond the growing gloom;
What catastrophes might be unfolding
On that slim, unstable stretch of water?

A headless chicken on *Rocksalt*'s roof
Reddens and revolves in sudden frenzy,
While in the ballroom along the road

A bingo caller hollers *"two fat ladies"*
To a sparse but satisfied assembly.

As the sun punctually dips down
Beyond the Jelly Mould Pavilion,
The receding tide meanders
Through the East Head gateway,
And the inner harbour boats
Collapse back on their sides.

When the Day Trippers Leave

When the tattoos are covered up
And unsightly bellies are put away.

When the swearing stops
Outside the harbourside pubs.

When the childrens' squeals
As they skip through the fountains
Turn to grumpy ingratitude.

When the car parks empty
And the trails of traffic cease.

When weary families
Slouch back up
The Old High Street.

When I can get a seat again
At *Steep Street Coffee House*.

When I no longer stumble over
Discarded chip boxes
And plastic beer glasses.

When the angry squawk
Of the constantly teased gulls
Is reduced to a plaintive mew.

When Harbour Arm food stalls
Are locked up for the night,
And music and laughter
Have faded into silence.

When the ghosts of
Hengist and *Horsa*,
And the *Orient Express*
Arouse my memory.

When the sun disappears
And dark clouds return,
And waves lash against
Precarious Copt Point rocks.

When the day trippers leave.

That is *my* time.

That is *my* Folkestone.

Notes on the Poems

When the Young Boy Arrived (apologies to Philip Larkin)
Final part in a trilogy of poems entitled *Folkestone's Golden Summers*, written as part of a project with the East Cliff Creatives group. Each poem was set sixty years apart.

A Writer's Town
Folkestone's regeneration has been founded largely on the visual arts, with writers relatively poor relations - this is an attempt to redress the balance.

Our Lady of the Harbour
In 2011, Cornelia Parker was commissioned to produce a statue for the second Triennial. Her inspiration was the Little Mermaid in Copenhagen harbour - with a twist. She wanted a "real person, a free spirit", not a young, idealised girl. Local mother of two, Georgina Baker, was selected.

Autumn Morning
Images from the fifteen minute stroll from my home on Radnor Park to the seafront.

Setting Sail for France
The first in the *Folkestone's Golden Summers* trilogy, recounting the day in 1843 when the railway was connected to the Harbour and the first packet boat carried passengers to France.

The Old High Street Awakens
Observations on the coming to life of the Old High Street on a typical Monday morning after a busy weekend.

I Sit in Coffee Shops
A piece of whimsy that describes my average day.

Sweet Pent Flow Softly
Charts the progress of the ancient watercourse from its source in the hills above the town to its outflow in the harbour. Although it was culverted in Victorian times to enable the building of a new shopping street, it still has the power to cause damage as the 1996 floods demonstrated.

Queueing for Potatoes
On 25th May 2017 a Gotha bomber dropped bombs on the area on the return to Germany from a fruitless raid on London. The devastation caused is detailed here.

Waiting for the Tide (A Gull's Life)
A daily ritual in the harbour.

Mermaid Beach at Dusk
Another dream sequence, this time focused on the pebble beach beneath the Leas.

Coffee Shop Devotional
Life in *Steep Street Coffee House*, dubbed the cultural hub of the Creative Quarter. Opened in 2015 by a young couple keen to run a Parisian style cafe.

Out on Bayle
The oldest part of town, home to the parish church and a proud community.

A Grand Opening

The second in the Folkestone's *Golden Summers* trilogy, describing the opening of what was originally named the *Grand Gentlemen's Mansions* in 1903.

A Path Fit for Heroes

The Zig Zag Path was built of Pulhamite between 1920 and 1921 by unemployed men on their return from the trenches.

Dust in my Cappuccino

Observed from the Lift Cafe, opposite which the first stage of building homes on the beach is underway. Closed since 2017, the reopening of the 1885 water lift is dependent upon a mix of National Heritage Lottery funding, community involvement and promised funding from the *Folkestone Harbour Company* on the sale of the first apartments.

Where Old Ghosts Meet

A dream sequence that touches on different characters, locations and events in the town's history.

East Cliff

Observations on an area overlooking the harbour with a long history.

The Seagull's Breakfast

An everyday pantomime performed outside coffee shops around town.

Triennial

A key element of the artistic regeneration engineered by former Saga owner and local benefactor, Sir Roger De Haan, has been an international art exhibition held every three years since 2008, though the fifth event, scheduled for 2020 was delayed until 2021.

Checkpoint George
An exploration of George Lane, just off Rendezvous Street, where traditional Folkestone "cafe culture" cohabits comfortably with its modern, more fashionable counterpart.

Breakfast at Marley's
Small, highly popular restaurant midway down the Old High Street on the site of *The Acropolis*, notorious honey pot for the youth of the town during the sixties and seventies.

Conversation with a Seagull
Says it all!

Sunday on the Harbour Arm
After many years lying derelict, following the closure of the railway, the Harbour Arm was renovated by the *Folkestone Harbour Company* and re-opened in 2015. On a warm summer's day there are few more popular places in the county. But the poem finishes on a cautionary note.

To Sit and Stare
Analysis of the importance of resting amid the current rush, and the availability of seating scattered around the town for that purpose.

The following seven poems reflect the experience of life under lockdown during the Coronavirus pandemic between March 2020 and late 2021:

On Sandgate Beachfront
A morning at Folkestone's coastal next door neighbour.

Sunscreen for the Apocalypse
The first lockdown, during which daily exercise was about the only thing permitted, coincides with a unseasonal heatwave.

Lake Life
And across town, things are also quiet in Radnor Park.

Abandoned Harbour
Wandering around a deserted harbour during lockdown.

Across the Muddied Park
Lamenting the gap of more than five hundred days between trips by rail to London for an erstwhile regular traveller with the station on the doorstep.

The Sea Pavilion (Casa Anacaona)
After eighteen months of restrictions preventing live music and theatre, this was one of the first public events to be held.

Burstin' Back into Life
Signs of a post-Covid world are emerging with the return of coach parties to stay in Folkestone's largest and most hotly debated hotel.

And finally.........

When the Day Trippers Leave
Sentiments shared by many local people.

ABOUT THE AUTHOR

Tony was born in Rochester in Kent in 1952, three days after tea rationing ended (an event almost as momentous for his mother as the birth of her only child). First taken on holiday by his parents to the coastal town of Folkestone at the age of ten, he returned more than half a century later to live.

With degrees in English and European and Anglo-Irish literature behind him, Tony had a thirty year career in civil service management (the last refuge of a modern day scoundrel), retiring in 2009.

He co-authored with Martin Moseling *A Half-Forgotten Triumph: The Story Of Kent's County Championship Title of 1913* to commemorate the centenary of the event, which was nominated for both the Wisden and Sports Book of the Year.

Since he moved with his wife to Folkestone in 2016, he has not only written and performed his poetry in a variety of locations, including coffee houses, bars and on the town's steep, cobbled Old High Street, but also created and managed a successful series of themed literary evenings, initially to cope with the first Covid-19 lockdown but still going strong after three years, and conducted award-winning walking tours of the local area.

This is his first collection of poetry.

Ingram Content Group UK Ltd.
Milton Keynes UK
UKHW010131040423
419518UK00003B/80